ocal selections

selections from

It's Only Life

a new musical revue

music & lyrics by
JOHN BUCCHINO

Cover design by Derek Bishop courtesy of PS Classics
Cover photo © Grace Weston

Visit John's website at
www.johnbucchino.com

ISBN 978-1-4234-5708-4

WILLIAMSON MUSIC®
A RODGERS AND HAMMERSTEIN COMPANY
www.williamsonmusic.com

EXCLUSIVELY DISTRIBUTED BY

HAL•LEONARD®

Visit Hal Leonard Online at
www.halleonard.com

© Jim Cox

AUTHOR'S NOTE

This songbook contains those songs from the musica
revue *It's Only Life* which are not already included in my
first songbook, "Grateful, The Songs of John Bucchino."

Many of the people who facilitated that first book are
also responsible for this one. Foremost among them is
my dear friend Mario Vaz De Mello who has patiently
helped me to get the exact notes and rhythms I intend
onto these pages. Mario, a wonderful composer in his
own right, has my boundless gratitude for his expert and
meticulous care.

Next, huge thanks to Daisy Prince who put this revue
together with me, choosing and ordering the material and
then directing the show's first incarnations with brilliant
insight. Daisy is one of the smartest people on the planet
and I've come to believe she understands these songs
better than even I do.

This songbook would not exist without the generous
support of everyone at Williamson Music and the
Rodgers and Hammerstein Organization, especially
Maxyne Berman Lang. Thanks also to Mark Carlstein and
the folks at Hal Leonard for shepherding the book to its
completion, to Stephen Schwartz for his friendship and
wise counsel, to Tommy Krasker and Philip Chaffin a
PS Classics for recording the CD, to Grace Weston for
her magical cover photo, and to the legendary Sheldon
Harnick for his kind Foreword.

Many musician friends have pored over this music and
offered suggestions as to how we might communicate
it more clearly. They are: Christopher Denny, Jonathan
Summers, Brent Crayon, David Cornue, Tim Hester, Bruce
Pomahac and Vince Scuderi. Thank you, so much, dea
fellows! And thanks to the singers who have performed
these songs onstage and on the CD, for teaching me so
much about them.

To singers: Rests in the melody correspond to my preferred
places for breaths. Notes with an X notehead are to
be spoken, not sung—they're only written on different
pitches to suggest a shape for the spoken inflection.
Also, please sing the written backphrasing which is very
specifically notated to create a conversational feel and
emotionally serve the lyric. For more performance hints
refer to our *It's Only Life* recording.

To pianists: The chord symbols are only a vertica
approximation of what is essentially a horizonta
contrapuntal flow. So, as much as possible, please play
the notes rather than relying on the chord symbols.

Finally, thank you, dear reader, for literally breathing life
into these songs. I hope they bring pleasure to you and
your listeners!

John Bucchino
New York, 2008

FOREWORD

John Bucchino is a remarkable songwriter. If you purchased this collection of his songs, most likely you know that already; if you are simply browsing through this songbook out of curiosity, you have an exciting discovery ahead of you. What will you find?

For one thing, you'll discover a unique voice, a voice like no other songwriter writing today. That distinctive voice is more than the sum of its parts, an amalgam of enviable gifts. To begin with, John is a true poet, with a poet's sensitivity to language and the ability to capture thoughts and feelings in memorable phrases. And when it comes to sharing those thoughts and feelings—including his worries, his anxieties, his desires—John is as fearless as he is candid. You'll discover songs that are intensely personal; yet to know these songs is to develop a sense of camaraderie with John: yes, I've thought that! I've felt that! I've experienced that!

He is a master craftsman but we're rarely aware of that aspect of his artistry; for John, the creation of a song seems as effortless and as natural as breathing. Anything he chooses to express, no matter how complex an idea, no matter how elusive a feeling, he manages to put into words and music. And as the thoughts and melodies pour out of him in what seems to be a free flowing stream of consciousness, instead of creating verbal and musical chaos, he invariably finds musical forms which make everything coherent. (Not only that: engaging rhymes keep popping up, often where you least expect them. Likewise, morsels of John's wry wit.) What else will you discover? A wonderfully rich harmonic palette and a melodic gift which enables him to give us music of ineffable tenderness as well as music of sheer animal excitement (along with everything that falls between those two extremes).

Enough. The songbook is in your hands; the songs are waiting to be relished. Expect the unexpected. John Bucchino is a remarkable songwriter.

Sheldon Harnick
New York

THE ARTIST AT 40

Words and Music by
JOHN BUCCHINO

PAINTING MY KITCHEN

Words and Music by
JOHN BUCCHINO

14

16

PLAYBILL

Words and Music by
JOHN BUCCHINO

LOVE QUIZ

Words and Music by
JOHN BUCCHINO

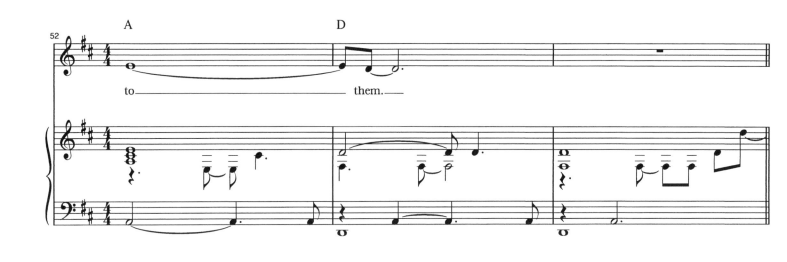

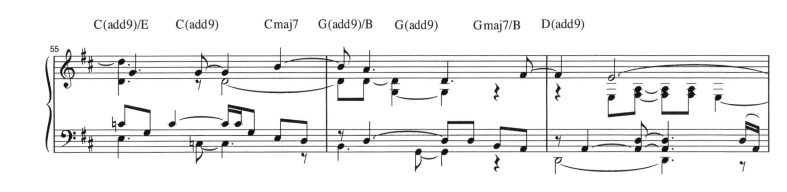

I know you al-ways feel— you've fal-len short, let— me down. You're wrong, you

A CONTACT HIGH

Words and Music by
JOHN BUCCHINO

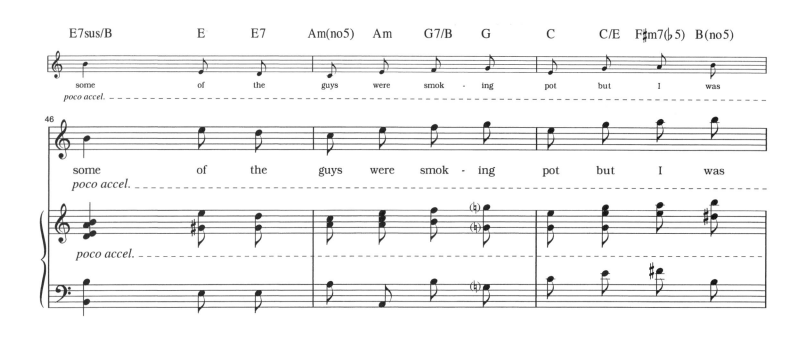

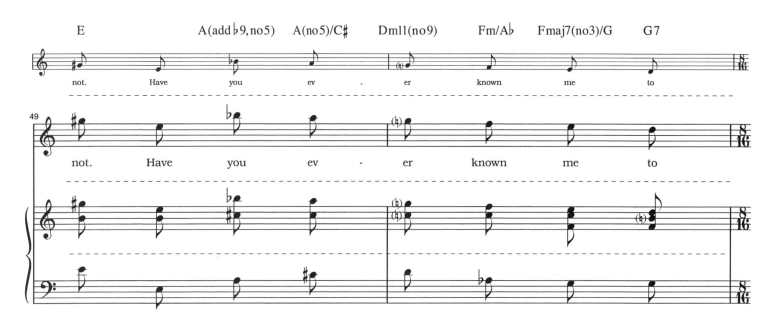

Poco piu lento (♪ = *250*)

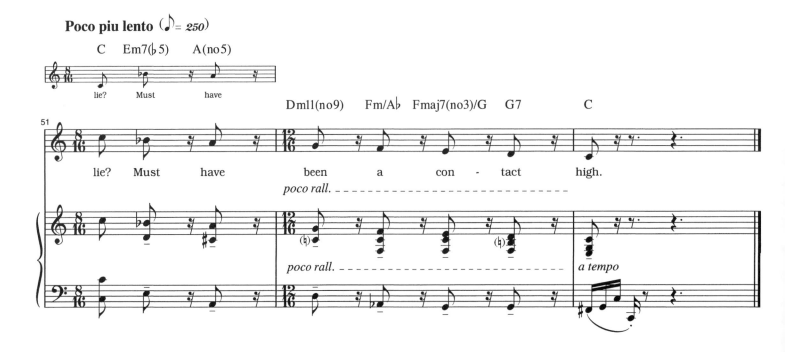

WHAT YOU NEED

Words and Music by
JOHN BUCCHINO

52

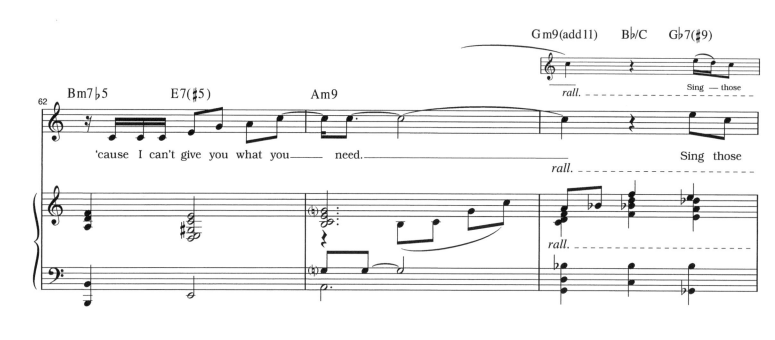

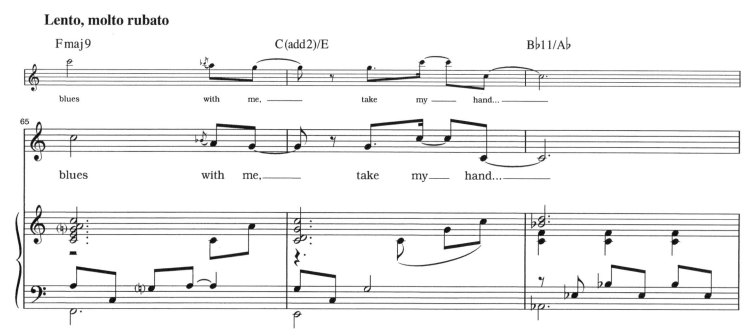

Lento, molto rubato

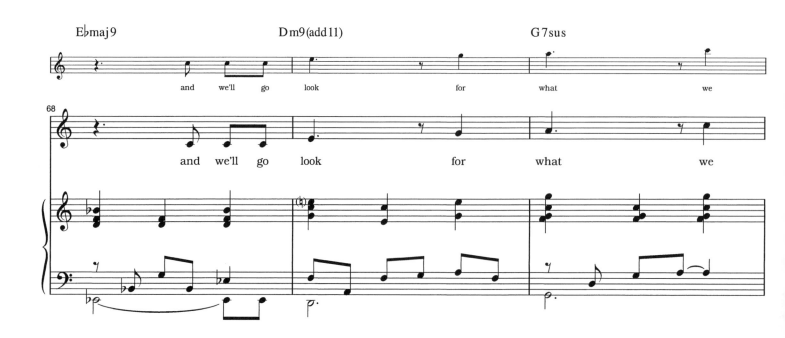

WHEN YOU'RE HERE

Words and Music by
JOHN BUCCHINO

Smoothly but with bounce (♩. = 114)

With pedal

Like ask-ing an oys-ter to cough up the pearl, the pry-ing on-ly makes

it shut—— tight - er.—— You,—— my friend, are a

58

62

I'M NOT WAITING

Words and Music by
JOHN BUCCHINO

PROGRESSION

Music by
JOHN BUCCHINO

With a steady, easy bossa-nova pulse

IT'S ONLY LIFE

Words and Music by
JOHN BUCCHINO

Robotic (♪ = *284*)

Suddenly Bouncy, Beatlesque (*Swung Eights*)

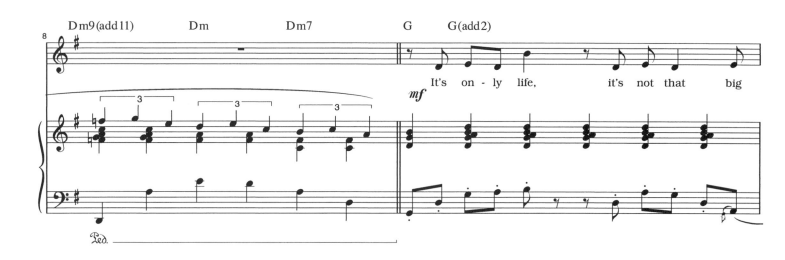

It's on-ly life, it's not that big a deal. A skin we shed, and once we're dead it does-n't mat-ter

(Bouncy)

un - less we want it to...

It's on - ly life, it's not that big

a deal. It's on - ly life, it's not that big

a deal. It's on - ly life.

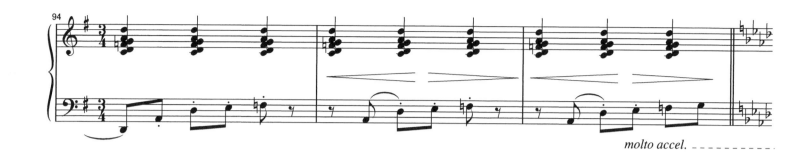

molto accel. ----------

Straight Eights

Piu mosso ($\quarternote = 160$) ($\eighthnote = \eighthnote$)

A♭6(add9)   A♭maj9(no3)   A♭maj7   A♭(add9)   A♭(add9,no3)

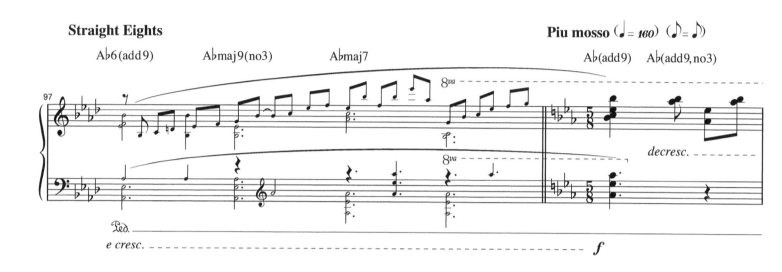

decresc. ----------

Ped. ----------

e cresc. ---------------------------- *f*

mp

Tempo I, Bouncy (*Swung Eights*) ($\eighthnote = 284$)

A(add2)   Em7(add11)   /G

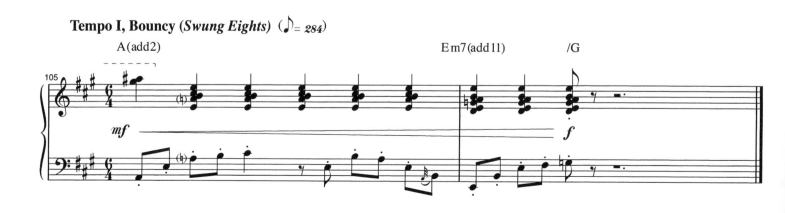

mf ----------   *f*

LOVE WILL FIND YOU IN ITS TIME

Duet for Tenor and Soprano

Words and Music by
JOHN BUCCHINO

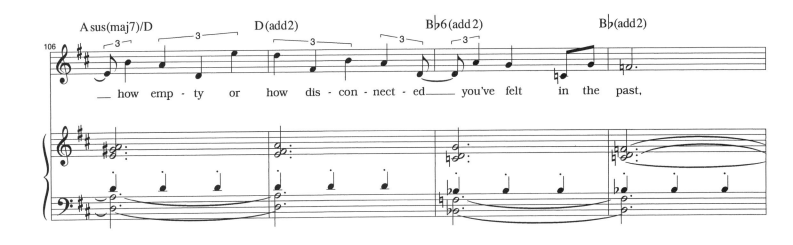

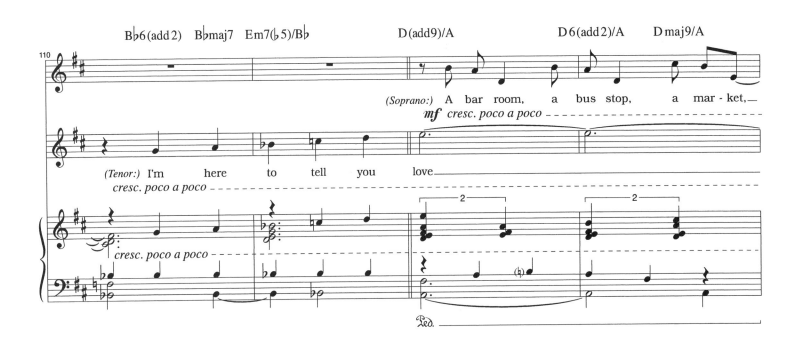

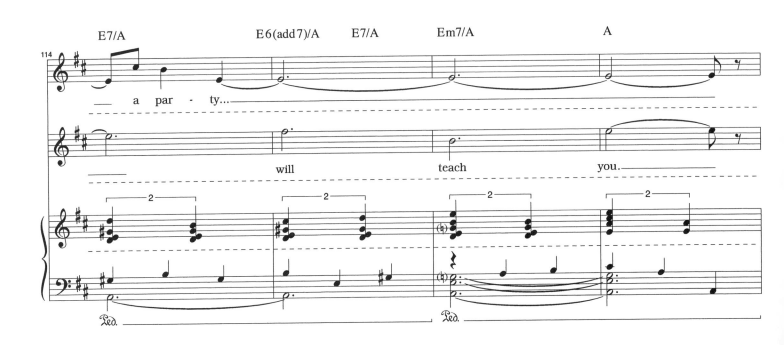

ON MY BEDSIDE TABLE

Words and Music by
JOHN BUCCHINO

* No Chord

I'VE LEARNED TO LET THINGS GO

Words and Music by
JOHN BUCCHINO

110

A GLIMPSE OF THE WEAVE

Words and Music by
JOHN BUCCHINO

116